SECULAR

Soprano solo and SATB unaccompanied

OXFORD

When I am laid in earth

'Dido's Lament' from
Dido and Aeneas

Henry Purcell

Arranged by
Stanley M. Hoffman

MUSIC DEPARTMENT

OXFORD

UNIVERSITY PRESS

When I am laid in earth

('Dido's Lament' from *Dido and Aeneas*)

Nahum Tate
(1652–1715)

HENRY PURCELL (1659–95)
arranged by Stanley M. Hoffman

Duration: 4 mins

OXFORD UNIVERSITY PRESS, MUSIC DEPARTMENT, GREAT CLARENDON STREET, OXFORD OX2 6DP
The Moral Rights of the Arranger have been asserted. Photocopying this copyright material is ILLEGAL.

When I am laid, am laid in earth, May my wrongs cre-ate No trou-ble, no trou-ble in thy

ah!_____ for - get my fate. Re-

ah!_____ for - get my fate. Re -

ah!_____ for - get my fate. Re -

ah!_____ for - get my_____ fate. Re -

delicatamente

ah!_____ for - get my_____ fate. Re -

-mem - ber me, but ah!_____ for - get my___

sub. **pp**

-mem - ber,___ but ah!_____ for - get___ my _____

sub. **pp**

-mem - ber,___ but ah! for - get my

sub. **pp**

-mem - ber,___ but ah!_____ for - get my___

sub. **pp**

-mem - ber,___ but ah! for - get my_____

Music originated by Andrew Jones
Printed in England by Halstan & Co. Ltd, Amersham, Bucks.

ISBN 978-0-19-353523-7

9 780193 535237